HEART OF THE HOME

THE MID-TWENTIETH CENTURY witnessed an historic change in kitchen design. Within the space of a single lifetime the functional back-stairs area of the house underwent a butterfly-like transformation into the colourful heart of the home. In a special fourteen-page kitchen supplement published in February 1953, *Picture Post* marvelled at how

> [t]he modern housewife's kitchen would have astonished her grandmother. Instead of the dark, ill-ventilated cave which *she* knew, the kitchen of today is light, airy, and highly equipped. Its separate components are carefully planned to make a complete, working unit. It is gracious, comfortable and efficient. Or it should be!

Gone was the Victorian model of a room inhabited by paid staff and set apart from family life. Social changes contingent upon two world wars and rapid technological advance had fundamentally changed expectations of who used the kitchen and what activities took place there.

By the end of the Second World War servants had virtually disappeared. The great pool of cheap female labour that had sustained the British tradition of domestic service, allowing even lower-middle-class households to employ a maid in 1900, had dried up in the face of more attractive employment opportunities. Girls who emerged from munitions factories after the First World War did so with a growing sense of their own capabilities. That they favoured the relative freedom of factory, clerical or shop work meant the 'Servant Problem' became a much-debated issue of the 1920s and 1930s. Upper- and middle-class wives who had not foreseen themselves entering the kitchen other than to give instructions now learnt how inefficient they had allowed their domestic arrangements to become and the notion of labour-saving aids began to gain popular currency. In the wake of the Second World War the impetus to improve kitchens was greater still as full employment and rising living standards contributed to a major social levelling. A steadily increasing proportion of married women opted to stay

Opposite:
An archetypal vision of the 1950s family. Father arrives home to find the mother of his two children cooking dinner in their bright, labour-saving kitchen.

in paid employment alongside their unmarried sisters and although an outside job did not negate the rigid assumption of kitchen as feminine space it did supply money to pay for gadgets and appliances that could ease the burden of work.

The women who returned to family life post-war or started out as housewives for the first time, whether middle or working class, now shared the common status of home labourer. Society encouraged them to take satisfaction in perfecting their domestic skills despite the potentially endless routine that came from combining the roles of cook, dishwasher, laundress, cleaner, nurse and hostess. As a result, when prosperity returned to Britain in the 1950s, the kitchen assumed greater prominence in household purchasing decisions. A 1950 editorial in *Woman's Own* proclaimed,

> This is the room more than any other you love to keep shining and bright ...
> A woman's place? Yes, it is! For it is the heart and centre of the meaning of home. The place where, day after day, you make with your hands the gifts of love.

The 1952 kitchen-dining room of a house at Chipping Field, the first estate built at Harlow New Town, Essex. The simple white wooden cupboards of post-war local authority housing were practical but lacked the streamlined glamour of later fitted units.

THE 1950s KITCHEN

Kathryn Ferry

SHIRE PUBLICATIONS

Published in Great Britain in 2012 by Shire Publications
Ltd, Midland House, West Way, Botley, Oxford OX2 0PH,
United Kingdom.

44-02 23rd Street, Suite 219, Long Island City, NY 11101,
USA.

E-mail: shire@shirebooks.co.uk   www.shirebooks.co.uk

© 2011 Kathryn Ferry. First printed 2011. Reprinted
2012.

A CIP catalogue record for this book is available from the
British Library.

Shire Library no. 627.   ISBN-13: 978 0 74780 827 5

Kathryn Ferry has asserted her right under the Copyright,
Designs and Patents Act, 1988, to be identified as the
author of this book.

Designed by Tony Truscott Designs, Sussex, UK
and typeset in Perpetua and Gill Sans.

Printed in China through Worldprint Ltd.

12 13 14 15 16   11 10 9 8 7 6 5 4 3 2

COVER IMAGE
Although this 1958 image is advertising gas-powered
appliances the incidental details are just as important.
Note the shiny utensils hanging up next to the cooker, the
aluminium saucepan with red plastic handle and the
examples of glass oven-to-tableware.

TITLE PAGE IMAGE
Food in this 1954 advertisement has been deliberately
chosen to associate Paul Kitchens with the emerging
interest in continental cookery. Bright red tomatoes are
reflected in the stainless steel worktop while aubergines
and tins of macaroni and bouillon sit on the table.

CONTENTS PAGE IMAGE
Although Tupperware was not introduced from the United
States until the 1960s, British women could buy plenty of
home-manufactured plastics. Transparent containers, like
the one in this rather saucily captioned advertisement,
showed their contents while boasting 'gay fitted lids to
brighten shelves'.

ACKNOWLEDGEMENTS
For their help sourcing material and images I would like to
thank Fred Gray, Elain Harwood, Derek Sugden, Jo Ward
at Stevenage Museum, David Devine at Harlow Museum,
Science Museum Archive, Institution of Engineering and
Technology Archive, Abraham Thomas and Richard
Westland.

I would also like to thank the people who have allowed me
to use illustrations which are acknowledged as follows:

The Advertising Archive, page 4; Birds Eye Iglo Group
Limited, page 62 (top); Daily Mail, pages 7, 16 (top right)
and 26; Derek Sugden, page 8 (top); Elsevier, images taken
from Home Management, ed. Alison Barnes, 2 vols, George
Newnes, London, 1957, pages 15, 50 (bottom), 52
(bottom) and 58 (middle); Good Housekeeping, page 9;
Colin Hile, page 49; Hoover UK, page 36;
© IPC+Syndication, page 29; Leisure Sinks (AGA
Rangemaster Group), page 20; Museum of Harlow,
Harlow Council, pages 6, 32 and 37 (top); National Media
Museum/SSPL, page 34; Christine Reilly, page 19; Salter
Housewares, page 48 (top left); Stevenage Museum, pages
37 (bottom) and 62 (bottom); Stork, pages 56 (top right)
and 58 (top), and Vim, page 42, extracts are reproduced
by kind permission of Unilever; Xpelair, page 8 (bottom).

All other photographs are from the author's collection.

CONTENTS

Week ending January 19 1957   Every Wednesday Fourpence

JOHN BULL

Beginning this week

WOMAN AT THE WHEEL
by SHEILA VAN DAMM

My unforgettable days with the heroes of Budapest

by NOEL BARBER

It was an attractive vision after the disruption of wartime separations and as the housewife took up residence in the kitchen her husband, children and guests joined her there.

The post-war era generally saw a move towards greater informality in household arrangements and the severe housing shortage offered a unique opportunity for architectural design to reflect this social change. Enemy air raids had punctured the streets of British towns and cities – 475,000 homes were left destroyed or uninhabitable; a greater number again suffered significant damage – while the wartime surge in marriages ensured that this drastic reduction in supply was combined with an unprecedented increase in demand. As part of the government's recovery agenda local authorities embarked on ambitious building programmes, beginning with estates of temporary 'prefab' dwellings and including the creation, from 1946, of fourteen New Towns. Smaller houses became the norm, both because there was intense pressure on land, labour and building materials and because they were easier for the modern nuclear family to heat and manage. The function of rooms also came under scrutiny as planners sought to maximise the limited space available.

Working-class women had long experience of combined kitchen-living rooms but, higher up the social scale, the implication of not being able to afford separate spaces generated snobbery against eating food in the same place as it was prepared. This stigma disappeared after the war. Multi-purpose rooms were now deemed to be fashionably modern and open planning became a statement of contemporary architecture, most influentially promoted in the Californian Case Study Houses designed by the likes of Charles and Ray Eames and Pierre Koenig. Although their radical vision of free-flowing space in sophisticated glass boxes was too advanced for most British families, steps were taken to assimilate the kitchen better into the rest of the post-war house. In the Homes and Gardens Pavilion at the 1951 Festival of Britain a series of architect-designed kitchen-dining rooms suggested ways to achieve this using movable screens and folding walls. A more widely endorsed solution was the dining recess or breakfast nook divided from the cooking area by an open sideboard or shelf unit. Where the kitchen and dining room remained as distinct entities a serving hatch was a highly coveted innovation. Mrs Martha Long

The ground floor of an architect-designed house in Kent (*Daily Mail Book of House Plans*, 1955). A serving hatch connects the kitchen with the dining-living room and a utility room replaces the old-fashioned scullery.

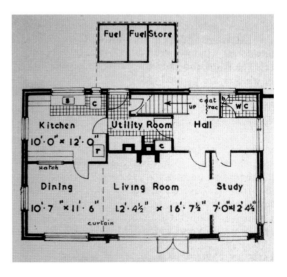

7

The open-plan kitchen designed by architects Peter and Alison Smithson for Sugden House, Watford, in 1956–7. The space works so well that few alterations have been made since it was built.

Opposite right: Open shelves were recommended as a way of separating the kitchen into distinct cooking and eating zones without cutting the housewife off from her family and guests. Rounded ends gave the unit a modern streamlined appearance.

Cooking smells were often cited as a downside of open-planning but extractor fans like this Xpelair were easy to fit and also removed excess condensation.

Our **XPELAIR**
cuts decorating costs
besides keeping the kitchen fresh

With an Xpelair in the kitchen you have less condensation ... far less damage to paintwork through walls running wet. The Xpelair whisks away steamy heat before it condenses. It removes cooking smells, gives quick relief from tiresome heat. Its shutter seals out draught when the fan is switched off. Next, no! The Xpelair has a new style outlet grille, unobtrusive, neat, pleasing.

Prices with shutter from £11.3.0; without shutter from £8.0.0. See the Xpelair at all good electrical suppliers or write for pamphlet PBI.

XPELAIR
DRAUGHTPROOF VENTILATION
XPELAIR, SALES, 31/32 HIGH HOLBORN, LONDON, W.C.1

watched the construction of her future home in a Hackney tower block and later recalled that, alongside the balcony, the serving hatch was the flat's chief attraction. Introduced during the 1920s to assist butlers in the easy service of meals and the rapid return of dirty dishes to the kitchen, by the 1950s serving hatches were in everyday family use, found in both private and council housing.

Basic services and fittings in the post-war kitchen represented a considerable improvement on the past. The Housing Advisory Committee's

1944 Dudley Report recommended as necessities a sink with draining boards, working surfaces, a ventilated larder and ceiling-height cupboards for dry goods and crockery. By 1958 one fifth of the population inhabited new houses built to these standards. The other four fifths, or 40 million people, did not. Many members of the baby-boomer generation remember childhood baths in the kitchen's old-fashioned Belfast sink as well as the cold floors and long wash days of a modernising but not yet modern era. The dream and the reality of 1950s kitchens could be a long distance apart. And yet it was an era of decisive

In multi-purpose rooms flooring could be used to differentiate spaces that were no longer formally defined by walls. The two linoleum patterns in this advertisement accentuate the existence of a fashionable built-in breakfast nook.

change. As house forms became standardised and economic differences between people narrowed, signs of individuality were displayed through the acquisition of luxury goods, often in the pursuit of the American-inspired dream of a fully automated fitted kitchen, held up as the ideal for all aspirant housewives and relentlessly pushed through glossy advertisements laden with exclamation marks. Owing to rising incomes and new mass-production techniques, this became increasingly affordable as the decade progressed, a sign of Harold Macmillan's famous election-winning claim that the British people had 'never had it so good'.

If your kitchen is to be beautiful but practical . . .

You need the Expert's help. Your kitchen must be planned and equipped by the expert — the man who understands and appreciates the housewife's problems as well as her good taste. This is just what Finch can do for you. A visit to our showrooms will prove to you conclusively that Finch planned kitchens are not only pleasing to the houseproud eye but also essentially practical and labour-saving. Pay a visit to our Showrooms at Finch Corner, Eastern Avenue (Southend Road), Ilford, Essex, and see for yourself the kind of kitchen you could have; or write for full particulars to B. Finch & Company Ltd., Belvedere Works, Barkingside, Essex. Nearest Tube Stations: Newbury Park and Gants Hill (Central Line). *Tel.: VALentine 8888 (30 lines)*

In this advertisement the fitted units by Finch are seen bathed in light through the all-important serving hatch. The foreground coffee pot and cups hint at the distinction between formal and informal dining on either side of the shuttered opening.

11

THE FITTED KITCHEN

THE POST-WAR fitted kitchen felt modern because of its coherence; unified cupboards made full use of wall space above and below a single work surface while flush finishes eliminated unhygienic dust traps. It saved labour because everything was thought through in advance. Appliances were slotted into the overall scheme and utensils were stored easily to hand. By the 1950s, kitchen design had found a place in popular culture and whether it was discussed in architectural journals, women's magazines, household manuals or recipe books the emphasis was always on proper planning. The look became more sleek and glamorous as the decade wore on, making kitchens as subject to changing fashions as the women with pinched-in waists who inhabited American-style advertisements selling the dream.

As a concept, the fitted kitchen had a long gestation period. In the mid-nineteenth century American writer and domestic goddess Catherine Beecher questioned the conventional layout and proposed her own 'model kitchen' designed according to a systematic assessment of tasks undertaken there. Ahead of her time, Beecher's ideas were later pursued under the banner of 'ergonomics', the avowed goal of which was to design the job, equipment and workplace to fit the worker. In 1913, fellow American Christine Frederick published the results of a ground-breaking time and motion study that measured the kitchen's efficiency by the standards of Henry Ford-style industrial productivity. The implication that it should be treated as the workshop of the home influenced kitchen design thereafter, with momentum shifting to Europe after the First World War. Modern Movement architects took up the challenge and in 1926–7 Margarete Schütte-Lihotzky's design for a fully fitted kitchen was installed in ten thousand Frankfurt flats. Inspired by the compact galley kitchens of contemporary ships and trains, the Frankfurt Kitchen rationalised every aspect of the housewife's routine to the point of providing storage chutes with handles so that there was no need to open cupboards and empty jars. Measuring just 68.5 square feet and defined by a strict functionalism, the Frankfurt kitchen was not suitable for the

Opposite:
To prove how affordable this Hygena kitchen could be, the prices were listed for each individual unit. A totally new look was yours for £90 but, as this advertisement stressed, the units could also be bought piece by piece.

average family home but its integrated fittings did suggest a way forward.

Research carried out by Lever Bros Ltd in the 1930s demonstrated that the decisive factor in saving labour was not square footage but the way in which the component parts of the kitchen were arranged. Their experiments aimed to determine the optimum room size for expending the minimum effort when cooking the very British menu of soup, fish and chips and apple pie, while washing clothes for a family of four. Although a bigger space increased the distances travelled, simply reducing the size did not reduce the work. The kitchen cabinet, pioneered in the mid-1920s by Liverpool-based firm Hygena, offered a partial solution. Designed to supersede the traditional open dresser, this new form of multi-purpose furniture was craftsman-built in wood and featured storage drawers, bins and cupboards *plus* a pull-out or pull-down work surface. Designs became increasingly complex in the 1930s, including fold-out ironing boards and even tables and benches, until the most expensive bespoke cabinets filled an entire wall. Though the most expensive examples were almost equivalent to a fitted kitchen, the basic free-standing cabinet remained sufficiently popular to become a common sight in many 1950s homes.

Post-war prefabs developed the cabinet idea into a single 'heart' unit integrating kitchen fittings and bathroom plumbing. Manufactured off-site to Ministry of Works specifications, the kitchen side of this back-to-back spine boasted a fitted work surface with the mod cons of cooker, wash boiler and

Opposite page: This American advertisement shows the sort of kitchens available in the USA in 1952. Complete with new Brunch-Bar and revolving Handy Pantry, the promise of a kitchen that could 'Save 1,000 steps a day' was the stuff of dreams for British housewives.

The progress of kitchen design from the open fire to fitted units, as depicted in a book of 1957. The pace of change quickened from the 1930s (third from top) through the 1940s and 1950s (top two illustrations).

15

Right: Everything in this factory-assembled ALPLA kitchen was made of aluminium or plastic. Designed by Gaby Schreiber in 1946 it was shown at home exhibitions into the 1950s, but never went into commercial production.

Below: A typical 1950s kitchen cabinet made of plywood with Formica-topped pull-down work surface. Now repainted, it stands in the author's kitchen.

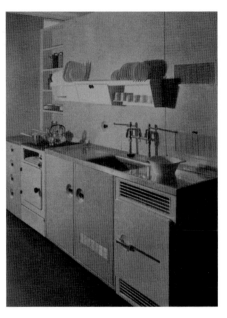

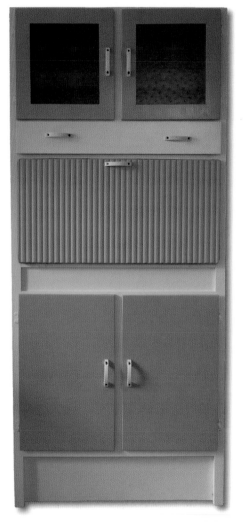

refrigerator arranged along it in an efficient sequence. With limited money, space and construction time, planning was reduced to the fundamentals of logical layout and sensible storage and, for ordinary people moving from the shared facilities of rented 'rooms' in the late 1940s, it was a real boon. Austerity conditions persisted into the first half of the next decade, so council tenants were among the earliest beneficiaries of kitchen improvements. In 1952 Peggy Miller got a brand new flat in Portobello Court, North Kensington, complete with 'the most beautiful modern kitchen, you know cupboards everywhere, and a double sink, and of course we had a brand new cooker ... and lovely working tops ...' Pre-war fittings, by contrast, had been limited to a couple of shelves, a sink and a draining board.

Numerous scientific trials were undertaken in Britain, the United States and Scandinavia to capitalise on the labour-saving potential of fitted kitchens and by the early

1950s the housewife's key tasks had been identified as food preparation, cooking and washing up, each linked to what became known as 'work centres'. Tests throughout the decade showed that the relationship between these centres determined mileage walked in the kitchen, so formulating an ideal 'triangle' between work surface, cooker and sink could substantially reduce unnecessary footsteps. Unfortunately, the location

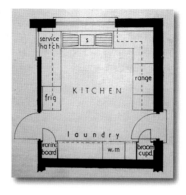

When planning or re-planning a kitchen, the unbroken 'U' plan was deemed to offer the most practical arrangement for work centres, with the sink as mid-point.

of key fixtures was frequently beyond the housewife's control and even moving into a new home was no guarantee of an ideally planned kitchen. In 1953 the Building Research Station examined the efficiency of kitchens designed by Powell & Moya for local authority flats in the Churchill Gardens Estate in Pimlico, London. Researchers not only claimed that a few simple changes in layout could reduce the distance occupants travelled by an average 18 per cent; they also managed to make space for a table and chairs to convert the working kitchenette into a more popular kitchen-dining room. In 1961 the government-sponsored Parker Morris Report, *Homes for Today and Tomorrow*, advocated as the culmination of the past decade's thinking a 'work sequence standard' of: work surface; cooker; work surface; sink; work surface. According to this plan, perfection was achieved in the U-shaped kitchen where no door or other traffic way broke the sequence. Seeking to influence builders in the private as well as the public housing sector, the report pointed out that only 5 per cent of existing kitchens satisfied this ideal.

Older houses had, of course, been planned according to different criteria. If this meant it was impossible for most

Most manufacturers offered a kitchen planning service. From 1953 the English Rose consultant produced blueprints and coloured drawings to help customers visualise their old-fashioned room (top left) modernised with fitted aluminium units.

17

A Beatall U.25 kitchen unit with Wareite worktop, fitted bread bin, cutlery drawer and shelves. Approved by the Council of Industrial Design, it cost £18 8s 1d in 1957 and was available in a choice of colours.

householders to realise the ultimate model of kitchen efficiency, major improvements could nonetheless still be made. Women were advised to list their daily jobs and scrutinise the movements required for each. Establishing an effective work flow was the first priority and, as the housewife spent most time there, the sink was often taken as the starting point. This should ideally be stainless steel, located under the window for good light. The cooker should be situated nearby but not in a corner or near a draught. If a woman was lucky enough to have both refrigerator and larder these should be together in one food storage zone. As far as preparation surfaces were concerned, a table could be useful for certain jobs but placing it in the centre of the room created unnecessary cross-kitchen traffic. Experts frequently advised its total

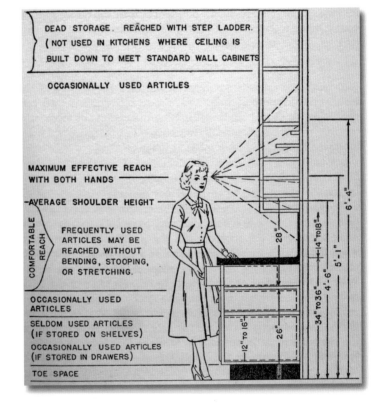

Diagram showing recommended heights for fitted units. Sight lines for the average woman standing at the work counter are shown in dotted lines with storage suggestions on the left.

replacement by fitted worktops, with the proviso that a toe space of at least 2 inches was left underneath cupboards to guard against backache.

Abundant storage was the great benefit of a fitted kitchen and with proper planning each work centre could be fully equipped with all the tools likely to be needed there. To be truly labour-saving, however, the units had to be at the correct height. In 1953 researchers at Cornell University in the USA monitored female subjects, who carried out their daily chores wearing metered oxygen masks to measure how much energy they expended in reaching, bending and stretching. Their results, which showed that bending

View of the original 1958 fitted kitchen in an 'Avon' bungalow on the estate developed by E. & L. Berg at Sunbury on Thames, Middlesex. Above the serving hatch that links kitchen and lounge are angled wall cupboards with sliding doors.

The name and imagery suggested that the housewife who bought a Leisure kitchen saved so much time she could put her feet up.

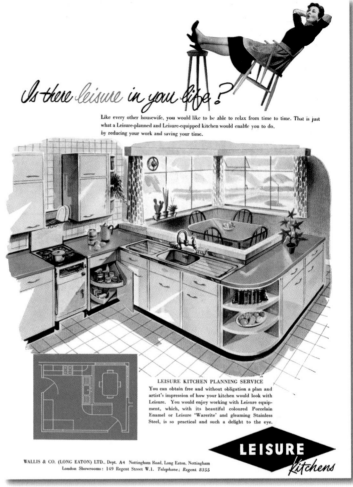

Is there leisure in your life?

Like every other housewife, you would like to be able to relax from time to time. That is just what a Leisure-planned and Leisure-equipped kitchen would enable you to do, by reducing your work and saving your time.

LEISURE KITCHEN PLANNING SERVICE
You can obtain free and without obligation a plan and artist's impression of how your kitchen would look with Leisure. You would enjoy working with Leisure equipment, which, with its beautiful coloured Porcelain Enamel or Leisure 'Warerite' and gleaming Stainless Steel, is so practical and such a delight to the eye.

LEISURE *Kitchens*

WALLIS & CO. (LONG EATON) LTD., Dept. A4 Nottingham Road, Long Eaton, Nottingham
London Showrooms: 149 Regent Street W.1. *Telephone;* Regent 8355

below counter height for pots and pans was more tiring than reaching up, led to the concept of 'comfortable reach', or the best height at which to store frequently used items, calculated to be between 30 and 60 inches from the floor. In their 'House of the Future', exhibited at the Ideal Home Exhibition in 1956, architects Peter and Alison Smithson designed a kitchen where almost all the fittings were built-in *above* waist level. Projecting the most modern thinking of their own time on to this vision of twenty-five years hence, they also gave the eye-level cupboards shallow compartments for ready accessibility. As the number of firms producing fitted units increased, dimensions became standardised so that by 1953 *Picture Post* could reassure readers that 'even though you may have bought two cupboards at two different times from two different shops, you will find, when they are put together, that they provide continuous, uniform working surfaces.' Unfortunately, as the *Architectural Review* pointed out in the same year, British Standard dimensions for appliances including cookers, refrigerators and washing machines did not relate to those recommended for kitchen fitments. This anomaly was gradually removed over the course of the decade.

Post-war interest in kitchen planning increased alongside the expansion of the manufacturing sector. Built-in units were previously available only to those who could pay an architect to design them and a joiner to make them. Technological advances during wartime stimulated the development of factory production, which meant members of the public could now choose

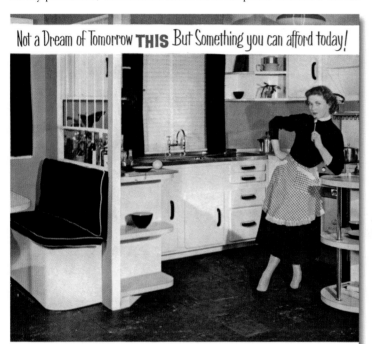

Not a Dream of Tomorrow THIS But Something you can afford today!

The Redwing Kitchen lends wings to work

The Redwing Kitchen is so much more than a kitchen—it's a kitchen, store-room, cafeteria, nursery, all rolled in one! First, and above all, it's PRACTICAL. Its gleaming working surfaces are proof against anything from spilled fat to mischievous children. Its cupboards are strategically placed—nothing is more than a pace away. Second, it's gay and cheerful—designed individually for you in your favourite colours. Most important of all, you can *actually afford it*. Easy Terms arranged with Redwing distributors enable you to start planning now!

Send for Free Coloured Leaflets . . . AND KITCHEN PLANNING CHART
You'll be surprised how easy it is to have a Redwing Kitchen. Just post a card addressed to Eileen Colls, our Domestic Consultant. She will send you full details of our Free Planning Service as well as news of remarkably painless easy terms.

Miss Eileen Colls, DEPARTMENT D2   **REDWING LIMITED, 340 Bensham Lane, Thornton Heath, Surrey**

The advertising copy accompanying this image encapsulates the 1950s kitchen as a multi-purpose living space. The Redwing kitchen is also a 'store-room, cafeteria [and] nursery, all rolled into one!'

VIVIEN LEIGH chooses a

PAUL
GUARANTEED
KITCHEN

The impeccable taste, the gleaming beautiful colours and the innate quality of Paul Kitchen Equipment led Vivien Leigh (Lady Olivier) to make it her choice. For her, and for every woman, there is infinite satisfaction in owning and using kitchen equipment of superb lifetime quality.

W. H. PAUL LIMITED
BREASTON · DERBY

London Showrooms   7 Royal Arcade
Old Bond Street   ·   London, W.1

Every piece Guaranteed Rustproof

142

Celebrity endorsements were a common way of glamorising fitted kitchens. This advertisement encouraged Vivien Leigh fans to think that by choosing Paul stainless steel units they could share in her film- star lifestyle.

This 1957 magazine provided instructions on how to create built-in units around an existing sink. Ready-made, it would cost £40 but the home handyman could do the work for £15.

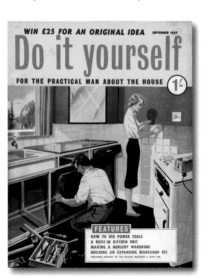

WIN £25 FOR AN ORIGINAL IDEA   SEPTEMBER 1957

Do it yourself

FOR THE PRACTICAL MAN ABOUT THE HOUSE   1/-

FEATURES
HOW TO USE POWER TOOLS
A BUILT-IN KITCHEN UNIT
MAKING A NURSERY WARDROBE
BUILDING AN EXPANDING WORKSHOP ETC

from a range of modular units, in metal as well as timber, prefabricated to fit together in any combination. Several companies transferred their production to kitchens from military aircraft. Feminine-sounding English Rose kitchens were produced from 1948 by CSA Industries of Warwick, who made use of stock-piled aluminium and the skills their workers had learnt pressing, bending and welding it during the war. Walthamstow cabinet-makers F. Wrighton & Sons diversified from bedroom furniture and radio cabinets into wooden kitchen units, having spent the conflict years making parts for the de Havilland Mosquito bomber.

Kitchens were a growth industry but mass production demanded a mass market. Manufacturers had to convince consumers that they needed to purchase new fittings, since kitchens had not traditionally attracted much spending. A post-war survey of young couples from Liverpool found that the greatest part of their furnishing budget was dedicated to the bedroom, followed by the dining room and living rooms, the kitchen accounting for between one eighth and one twentieth only. Rising home ownership encouraged investment – in the 1920s 90 per cent of

homes were still rented whereas by 1950 some 60 per cent were owner-occupied – but this was not enough on its own. Branding and advertising were crucial. The names chosen by manufacturers were calculated to imply certain enviable qualities: Leisure, Ezee and Nevastane suggested labour-saving; Wrighton chose to link its Californian range to the sunny home of contemporary design; and Fleetway of Edmonton, North London, sold its distinctive angled cupboards under the romantic trade names Florentine and Napoli. At the same time as portraying their products in overtly modern and aspirational terms, manufacturers were also at great pains to point out how affordable a fitted kitchen could be, particularly if it was bought a bit at a time.

If DIY was a step too far, self-assembly kitchen kits were available by the late 1950s. A precursor of modern flat-packed furniture, this Peerless 'Kitchen by Post' was delivered in sections that slotted together.

Displaying up-to-date tastes, however, did not have to involve moving to a new house or even buying a ready-made fitted kitchen. Pride in home ownership could just as easily be demonstrated by doing the work for oneself. People who had found personal satisfaction in following the wartime mantra of 'make do and mend' now discovered an enthusiasm for the latest hobby of DIY and the kitchen was one area where handywork could make a huge difference. The encyclopaedic book *Home Management*, published by George Newnes in 1957, advised:

> Standard hardboard is ideal for making 'built-in' or removable kitchen fitments of every description. Mounted on a timber framework by means of pins, screws, or … adhesive, hardboard panels give a good-looking result … Complete the job with matching accessories of contemporary style.

Building cupboards and boxing-in the sink were set forth as achievable projects and the new home-making magazines were full of promotions for innovative surfacing materials to finish the job.

COLOUR AND MATERIALS

MAKING THE KITCHEN a congenial place to work and spend time was crucial to transforming it into a family space. After the enforced drabness of wartime, colour invaded the home and women were encouraged to consider decoration as beneficial to their well-being. Advertisers and design commentators pushed the idea that household chores were more satisfying when undertaken in attractive surroundings, simultaneously stressing the labour savings possible with modern materials. As the petro-chemical age took off in earnest, fresh options were available to brighten every kitchen surface from the wall to the floor, embracing even the humble washing-up bowl. Countless products were launched on to the market tagged with upbeat Festival of Britain buzzwords such as 'colourful', 'light' and 'gay'. In 1951 the extensive use of primary colours throughout the South Bank exhibition pavilions heralded a new celebratory mood in design that was ultimately transferred to more domestic settings through paint and PVC, linoleum and laminates.

This shift was by no means immediate. The plastics that would ultimately be the key means of colouring the kitchen suffered a reputation problem in the immediate post-war years. Viewed as optimistically futuristic in the 1920s and 1930s, plastics were used in wartime to compensate for the scarcity of more traditional materials and became associated with fakery. On top of that, the surplus from military manufacture was used with too much haste to make products that were unable to withstand daily use. It took time to dispel these prejudices, just as it took time to shake off old ideas about colour. Modernist interiors had gloried in the hygienic virtues of white, valuing its clinical associations of precision, order and control. For ordinary inter-war kitchens, pastel tones proved easier to live with, the *Bride's Book* of 1939 declaring that 'with yellow, or cream or even white walls, there are a number of charming colour schemes for curtains which will help make this workshop of the home a pleasant place'. By 1953, however, writing in the *Daily Mail Ideal Home Book*, Annette Stockwell could still lament the lingering and entirely opposite tendency towards what she called the War Office attitude: 'So long as a colour

Opposite:
Curtains stitched from a cotton fabric like this, brightly patterned with the latest must-haves of 1950s kitchen design, were an easy way to add modern colour.

doesn't show the dirt it is a safe colour … the nearer it is to the colour of dirt the safer it is.' Hers was just one voice among many seeking to embolden the British public in their use of colour: 'a warm sunny room may suggest cool greys, light blues or greens, whereas a cold kitchen or one with a dull depressing outlook may demand warm colours, corals, pinks, acid yellows and stimulating reds.'

An illustration of Annette Stockwell's basement kitchen from the *Daily Mail Ideal Home Book*, 1953–4. Using coral and white paint, she turned the once dark storage area into a cheerful dining space, choosing sky blue and pale yellow for the working end.

Painting the walls was an inexpensive way to transform any kitchen, a task made easier by the introduction in the 1950s of polyvinyl acetate emulsions available under trade names such as Polimul, Pammastic and Berger's Magicote one-coat gloss paint. Interlight Emulsion and Interlux Contemporary Enamel came in a range of 'House and Garden' colours with mouth-watering names including Lemon Peel, Green Olive, Cantaloupe, Mocha and Aubergine, all calculated to evoke the exotic flavours beginning to enter post-war cooking. Owing to the advent of fluorescent lighting, it was possible to appreciate the choice of vibrant tones even in an old-fashioned basement kitchen. Contrasts were a positive virtue in contemporary styling, so anyone with doubts was advised to 'decorate the walls white and treat the incidentals, cupboards, or the odd recess, in bright colours'. Fitted units

'The artist's an acrobat too, I see'

'You can laugh, Jane, but it takes skill and experience to paint the kitchen while the little woman is spoiling the broth.' 'Never mind, darling, it looks gorgeously glossy and colourful.' 'This Brolac's very pleasant stuff to use I must say. Going a long way too.' 'Yes John, clever boy to choose it.'

'It'll last for donkey's years. Did you know that Brolac is specially made to stand up to steam?' 'No—honestly?' 'Hullo—I don't like that look in your eye, Jane. What's cooking?' 'Nothing really, I was just sort of—thinking—about the bathroom.'

BRIGHTEN YOUR HOME WITH BROLAC AND MURAC P·E·P

Colourcards from John Hall & Sons (Bristol & London) Ltd., Hengrove, Bristol 4.

Brolac was a specialist kitchen paint designed to stand up to steam. It was so easy to apply that the fictional 'John' in this advertisement could paint while 'Jane', otherwise described as 'the little woman', got on with the cooking.

were increasingly manufactured in a variety of colour-ways and the late 1950s saw a trend for 'Harlequin' mix-and-match combinations. Two-tone cupboards finished in a different colour either side of the obligatory drawer line remained popular well into the next decade.

Laminated plastic worktops were an easy way to add colour, whatever the budget. The leading brand of Formica was invented in 1913 and evolved from an insulating material into the ubiquitous surface treatment of post-war America. So high was demand that by the 1940s the company's Ohio factory stretched across a 22-acre site, its trademark heatproof sheets mass-produced by thermal-setting layers of paper impregnated with melamine resin. British company De la Rue secured the licence for UK and European production in

The Wrighton 'Californian' kitchen was launched in 1958 with a shiny new polyester lacquer finish called Decpol. Developed in collaboration with a German company, scratch-resistant Decpol came in eight 'gleaming' colours, '... far more hard-wearing than any paint finish'.

A 1950s book of Formica colour samples. 'Softglow', the pattern shown here, was a popular worktop choice among the makers of fitted kitchens.

1947, subsequently pursuing the successful US marketing strategy of promoting Formica's labour-saving qualities alongside its colourful look. This advertising copy from 1954 was typical:

> You'll be happy ever after when you have jewel-bright clean-at-a-wipe 'Formica' Laminated Plastic work-tops in your kitchen. A 'Formica' table alone cuts down your chores more than you would credit. This tough, satiny surface is lovely to look at and lovely to live with – for a lifetime. You simply can't make a mark on it without drastic misuse – it won't stain, won't chip, won't crack.

Durable yet inexpensive, Formica helped democratise modern design by bringing the latest colours and patterns into ordinary homes, gaining a reputation as *the* DIY product of the era. Its main competitor was Wareite,

An example of how to decorate with colour from the May 1959 issue of *Ideal Home*. To flatten out the walls of their historic Buckinghamshire kitchen Mr and Mrs G. G. Riddick lined them all with Formica.

manufactured by Bakelite Ltd at Ware in Hertfordshire, with other plastic veneers going by the names of Panax, Klingdecor and Perstop.

In addition, there were new adhesive-backed plastic fabrics publicised for their easy-to-apply transformative effects; why not, for example, 'Give the

An example of contemporary-styled linoleum. 'Gay, bold, distinctive' it certainly was, but this advertisement's claim that the Barbecue pattern was 'easy-to-live-with in any home' is harder to credit.

kitchen table a new gleaming surface. Go gay with Fablon.' Rival Marleyfilm was hailed as a popular vinyl asbestos wonder surface while Stix-On offered the cheapest alternative for covering shelves and draining boards. To decorate the wall in between worktop and cupboards, there were synthetic substitutes for the traditional ceramic tile. Congowall, the 'tile-look-a-like', came in brightly coloured glueable sheets that gave a tough glossy cellulose finish for less than 10 pence a square foot. There were also polystyrene wall tiles – Everine was available in eight different sizes and nine different colours:

... flawlessly moulded ... with bevelled edges and a glass-smooth finish. Putting them on is so simple – just squeeze five spots of adhesive from the tube onto the corners and centre of the tile then slide it into position. It couldn't be easier – the finished effect couldn't be lovelier!

THIS PATTERN IS **WILLIAMSON'S**

Barbecue

Gay, bold, distinctive – easy-to-live-with in any home. Choose it for decor and choose it for wear. Remember, nothing outwears linoleum!

'Barbecue' is only one of the many high quality, reasonably priced inlaid linoleums produced by Williamson's and stocked by leading stores.

'Barbecue' is available in red, grey and yellow. To help you get this pattern, cut out the coupon opposite and take it to your shop.

TAKE THIS PATTERN TO YOUR SHOP AND ASK FOR
WILLIAMSON'S 'BARBECUE' IN RED (6693) GREY (6695) YELLOW (6694)

WILLIAMSON LINOLEUM

THELMA JAS. WILLIAMSON & SON, LTD · BARRY, OSTLERE & SHEPHERD LTD
DUNDEE LINOLEUM CO LTD · LINOLEUM MANUFACTURING CO LTD
MICHAEL NAIRN & CO LTD · NORTH BRITISH LINOLEUM CO LTD
SCOTTISH CO-OPERATIVE WHOLESALE SOCIETY LTD
–are all members of The Linoleum Manufacturers' Association

The era of cheerful, easy-clean surfaces also produced innovations in flooring. Materials such as tile, wood and stone gave way to polyvinyl chloride (PVC), cork, rubber and linoleum. Actually a Victorian invention, the last received a boost after 1956 when The Linoleum Manufacturers Association (THELMA) rose to the challenge presented by newer materials with a major marketing initiative and contemporary designs. Linoleum remained competitive because it could be purchased in various thicknesses and qualities, and, like PVC, was available as sheets or tiles. Laying two contrasting colours in a chequerboard effect proved particularly popular but these hard-wearing floor treatments could also be cut into customised patterns. Marbled designs offered a modern take on a traditionally expensive material while 'Harlequin' vinyl

tiles, added to the Marley range in 1955, mimicked terrazzo with multi-coloured spatters on a coloured background. 'Confetti', made by Morris Rubber Industries of Byfleet in Surrey, promised a similar effect and, though they were not grease-resistant like PVC, rubber tiles were a well-used alternative.

The kitchen window provided further decorative opportunities. Venetian blinds were all the rage – 'regulated at a touch to give perfect sunshine control or night-time privacy' – and so in harmony with the modern fitted

The salmon-pink and white kitchen of a new-build bungalow in Kent (1958). On the living-room side of the serving hatch/breakfast bar a red-and-white striped awning adds a contemporary twist.

With tubular steel legs and a plastic laminate top, the 1950s kitchen table was a world away from its heavy wooden predecessor. With plasticised vinyl upholstery, the matching chairs could also form part of the wipe-clean kitchen dream.

kitchen that readers of the *Daily Mail Book of Bungalow Plans 1958* were assured, 'Venetian blinds complete the picture of the happy housewife'. By this date 'plastic' curtain fabrics were also available for a refreshing new look: '… soft as kid leather, warm to the touch, easy to keep clean – they only require sponging and they are printed in delightful flower patterns and contemporary designs.' And in a space once too plagued by condensation for wallpaper, the new rolls with a washable vinyl finish and light-hearted designs became the ultimate way to add bold pattern. Often abstract, linear and stylised, kitchen wallpaper also developed a gloriously kitsch line in the representation of vegetables, herbs and fruit, which originated in the United States and was soon embraced in Britain as particularly appropriate to the room's uses.

The kitchen at No. 51 Northbrooks, Harlow, the 'Silicone' show home of 1957. Bold wallpaper with stylised illustrations of food represents the latest trend and a leap forward in design from New Town show homes earlier in the decade (see page 37).

No area of the kitchen was free from the onward march of plastics technology, allowing even the most utilitarian items to blend with the overall colour scheme. As the first example of domestic moulded hollow ware, the polythene washing-up bowl was greeted in 1948 with considerable scepticism. Slow but steady acceptance led on to the polythene bucket and a growing momentum for other products. Between 1948 and 1957

'Alkathene', the ICI brand of polythene used for household wares, rose from less than one per cent of the UK's annual polythene production to nearly 40 per cent. Housewives were guaranteed easy-to-clean hygienic products that were durable, rust-proof and noiseless in use. A 1960 article on the 'Domestic Revolution in Plastics' pointed out that 'They have the further asset of lightness; who would nowadays want to carry water in a heavy pail?' Women's magazines were liberally scattered

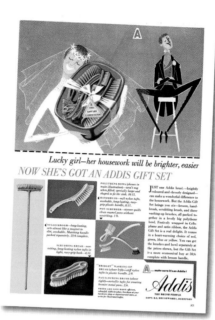

Coloured plastic washing-up bowls and brushes were such a novelty that they could be bought gift-wrapped to give as a wedding present. This Addis set came in a choice of red, green, yellow or blue.

with advertisements for the latest plastic kitchenware, from pedal bins by Fethaware, through EKCO colanders and sink-tidies, to storage containers and bread bins by Bex.

All this was part of a new emphasis on using well-designed everyday items to contribute to the contemporary kitchen aesthetic. Writing in *The Architectural Review* in 1953, Mary Ward suggested that 'china, glassware and spices in jars could be attractive if visible through glass [cupboard] fronts'. Carefully chosen displays on open shelves could also add interest. One of the most popular products used in advertising and show kitchens of the era was undoubtedly Cornishware, the famous blue and white banded pottery made by T. G. Green that struck just the right note of modern simplicity. Two-tone storage tins made by companies such as Tala were also designed to be seen, with their contents announced on the side in a brightly coloured typeface that matched the lid. The Metal Box Company sold similar stainless steel canisters under the Worcester Ware trademark, marketing them alongside more elaborate patterns. So all-embracing was this interest in brightening the 1950s kitchen that even the labour-saving appliances we now know as 'white goods' were available in a choice of differently coloured vitreous enamel finishes.

Worcester Ware was marketed as 'an inexpensive way of bringing colour in to the kitchen shelves!' Dating from the early 1950s, these tins prove claims of the time that their 'gay decoration' will 'remain bright and colourful for many years'.

33

LABOUR-SAVING APPLIANCES

F EW KITCHEN products were marketed in the 1950s without a promise to save labour. As British society became more affluent the relationship between time and money shifted in the public consciousness. During the decade the average weekly wage almost doubled from £6 8s 0d to £11 2s 6d while the standard rate of income tax fell by two shillings in the pound. Having previously been time-rich and money-poor, the average housewife increasingly questioned the drudgery of her long working week (a Mass Observation survey of 1951 estimated it as 75 hours, plus overtime on Saturdays and Sundays), succumbing to the widely dispensed notion that by investing in modern appliances she could literally buy herself leisure. Spending on domestic articles went up by 115 per cent overall and household items that had been viewed as luxuries began to take on the mantle of necessities. In 1945 just 2.1 per cent of households had an electric refrigerator and 3 per cent an electric washing machine. By 1965 those figures had risen to 46 per cent and 58 per cent respectively. Once the immediate post-war export drive subsided, mass production was directed to the home market, the modern concept of planned obsolescence emerging alongside the rapid expansion of choice in appliances.

Powering the technological advance of the 1950s was the clean, efficient energy of the future – electricity. Up to this point the supply network had been slow to expand, so pre-war houses were far more likely to rely on gas for lighting, cooking and heating water. Indeed the two fuels were in active competition throughout the 1950s, the Gas Board vigorously promoting its product with the aid of mascot Mr Therm. Electricity remained the more expensive option but by 1951 almost 90 per cent of all households were connected to the National Grid, the remainder benefiting from construction of the new supergrid over the ensuing decade. Praising its relative value for money in an annual feature on 'Living Electrically', the May 1956 issue of *Good Housekeeping* pointed out:

Opposite:
This 1950 studio photograph reinforces the idea that kitchen appliances were the housewife's best friend. Over the decade improvements in design and efficiency made the latest models increasingly desirable.

A comic take on labour saving!

For the cost of twenty cigarettes a day it does the washing, sucks dust from floors and furniture, cooks the meals, heats the water, preserves perishable foodstuffs, lights the house inside and out, and warms it within.

This 1950s Hoover advertisement could not be clearer in its message that modern appliances were a direct substitute for human servants. Despite this widely proclaimed view, large sections of housework simply could not be automated.

In the days before its use was taken for granted, creating the right labour-saving image for electricity was extremely important. There were also practical problems to overcome, not least of which was the fact that different appliances came with different plugs. By the mid-1950s standardisation was approaching owing to the development of ring main circuits fitted with three-pin plugs. In kitchens, however, there remained an issue about the number of sockets available for new appliances; the average for post-war new builds was just six *per house*.

When it came to cookers, efficiency had increased to such a degree that domestic commentators rarely favoured one fuel source above another, portraying the decision as one of personal choice. Careful consideration was, nonetheless, advised, the Newnes book of *Home Management* going so far as to state:

Choosing your cooking stove is a momentous event, second only to choosing your life partner. For you and the cooker you finally select from to-day's dazzling array will doubtless have to work together in harmony for many years to come.

In 1953 the average kitchen was thought to produce 1,000 cooked meals annually but manufacturers were only just beginning to standardise their thermostatic control settings. Until they did so, it was impossible for recipes to specify cooking times, making a woman's knowledge of her own stove crucial.

Left: Mod cons of 1953 in the Orchard Croft show kitchen at Harlow. In addition to the fridge and cooker, the electric wall clock and hot water boiler were desirable novelties.

Below: The Electrical Association for Women offered qualifications for female demonstrators who worked in Electricity Board showrooms like this one in Stevenage New Town. Note the latest range of cookers on display along the back wall.

HERE NOW

Automatic cooking... by Gas!

It's the most advanced gas cooker in Britain today!

THE FLAVEL **'Autocrat'**

switches itself on ... turns itself off
when the food is cooked

Just set the 'Autocrat's' automatic controls and forget about the cooking. Go shopping ... see a film. A hot meal will be waiting when you walk in the door, because the new 'Autocrat' switches itself on at the proper time ... turns itself off when the food is cooked. Instant-view oven control, beautifully-styled kitchen clock and 5-hour timer are set in a streamlined modern control panel with strip lighting. And every burner-hotplate, oven and grill lights *automatically* at the turn of a tap.

Exclusive BAKE-WARM control to big, light-reflecting oven (keeps food hot without drying) plus glide-over hotplate plus roomy storage drawer; plate warming compartment plus many more exclusive Flavel features make the 'Autocrat' wonderful value. See the 'Autocrat' at your local Gas Board Showrooms today. With new easier-than-ever H.P. terms you can have Britain's most advanced gas cooker installed in only a few days for a small initial deposit.

SEE A **FLAVEL** FIRST

SIDNEY FLAVEL AND CO. LTD · SALES DIVISION · EAGLE FOUNDRY · LEAMINGTON SPA · TELEPHONE 3091

Timer-control cooking was sold as the ultimate convenience. With the Flavel 'Autocrat' you could 'Go shopping ... see a film. A hot meal will be waiting when you walk in the door.' Advertisements glossed over the fact someone still had to prepare the food!

Gas cookers had the advantage of a visible flame with instantaneous control, lit by flash ignition instead of matches come the end of the decade. Electric cookers lacked fumes, so were often viewed as a cleaner alternative. Cooking with solid fuel was also an option, the old-fashioned range now transformed into the type of heat storage cooker-boiler epitomised by makers AGA (introduced from Sweden in 1929), Esse and Rayburn. All became more streamlined during the 1950s as makers responded to general trends in kitchen design. Welcome innovations included storage drawers in the plinths that replaced legs, larger ovens (space for a 22-pound turkey was the key measure) and drop-down doors. In 1953 Cannon launched the A125 gas cooker with fold-away eye-level grill, advertising it as 'the greatest advance of the century in cooking'. The glass oven door appeared in the same year: 'The Vulcan is the only gas cooker with this wonderful, worry-saving feature. Guaranteed fireproof and unbreakable, the Panel cannot steam over and retains full oven heat.'

Most modern of all were the cookers fitted with automatic control or 'robot' systems. The Creda Super Comet was Electric Cooker of the Year in 1954 with 'the oven that switches itself on – does the cooking – switches itself off!' Double-fronted, it came complete with a central, appropriately space age, control panel. As the idea of cooking by timer control grew more popular towards the end of the decade devices appeared which could be fitted to existing manually operated cookers.

Whereas everyone needed a cooker, the same was not yet true of a refrigerator. Demand increased substantially over the decade though it remained a long way behind the USA, where climatic conditions had inspired a much earlier take-up. In 1958, 97 per cent of US households had a refrigerator, compared to only 10 per cent in Britain. A turning point came that same year, however, when the April Budget halved purchase tax on refrigerators and all hire purchase restrictions were removed in October. Sales for 1958 hit a record high of 440,000. The Electrical

Association for Women's 1960 survey 'Electrical Viewpoint' confirmed a preponderance of sales over the previous two years, respondents showing a clear preference for the compressor rather than absorption type, with more than half owning a table-top model. Gas- and oil-powered refrigerators were also available, the choice of size and capacity improving generally throughout the 1950s.

Many people who lived in older houses outside urban centres still made do with the traditional larder but the tide of public opinion was being relentlessly turned in favour of refrigerators. They were built into the kitchens of post-war prefabs because they saved space and, until councils ran out of money, they were also fitted in local authority housing. The larder began to disappear from kitchen plans; in 1955 *The Daily Mail Ideal Home Book* confidently asserted that 'The new house or flat has [a refrigerator] installed as a matter of course, and the new housewife begins her catering life with it, never knowing the inconvenience of limp and not quite fresh foods and milk.' Not having to shop every day saved time while reduced food spoilage, combined with the ability to store and use up leftovers, saved

Mid-range refrigerators provided an additional worktop at unit height; this best-selling Prestcold model was made by the Pressed Steel Company of Cowley, Oxford. Regular defrosting was recommended once a fortnight.

39

The surprise of her life—and the best!

HERE's the finest present that ever surprised a wife. It's the ENGLISH ELECTRIC EA-83. Constantly, she'll be amazed and grateful for the things this gleaming beauty can hold — enough room inside to take a banquet. Why, even the door is a larder! Lots of refrigerated storage space means lots of advantages. You can do a week's food shopping in a day. You can plan your meals well ahead. Left-overs won't 'go off'. Cake mixes and vegetables can be prepared today and stored until required.

Here is the refrigerator to give you a fresh interest in food, more fun and more leisure. One more surprise. It only occupies just over 5 square feet of floor space — fits any moderate sized kitchen comfortably!

TO READ AND THINK ABOUT

More than 15 sq. ft. of adjustable shelf area — giant, full-width Freezer— special Coldrawer for meat and fish—two big Humidrawers for fruit and vegetables —and three generous shelves in the door itself! White or cream enamelled finish.

SEE IT TODAY

See the ENGLISH ELECTRIC EA-83 at your local ENGLISH ELECTRIC Authorised Dealer or Electricity Service Centre. Generous Hire Purchase Terms are available. Cash price £100.12.0. Purchase Tax extra.

'ENGLISH ELECTRIC'

BRINGING YOU BETTER LIVING

The ENGLISH ELECTRIC Co. Ltd.,
Domestic Appliance and Television Division, East Lancashire Road, Liverpool 10

Printed in England by Messrs. Bradbury, Agnew & Co., Limited, at 15-29, Phoenix Place, Mount Pleasant, W.C.1, and published by them weekly, with one additional Almanack issue, at 10, Bouverie Street, London E.C.4.—WEDNESDAY, May 25, 1955.

money, an estimated two to three shillings a week. Piling on the pressure, the Gas Council's compendious guide to *The Happy Home* stated as fact that 'Every housewife today aspires to own a refrigerator, which is indeed essential for the safe and satisfactory storage of perishable foods.' Concerns about food hygiene had been on the increase since certain preservatives were banned in 1928 and from that time on advertisements for refrigerators began to prey on fears of unseen decay. The housewife who was unmoved by potential labour-saving benefits could not be so heartless as to neglect her loved ones' well-being because, as a 1959 Prestcold promotion declared, 'a refrigerator affects the *health* of the family. In an ordinary larder germs multiply fast – even in winter. But food in a refrigerator is safe food, because it is kept cool enough to prevent the action of bacteria.' A modern kitchen was a healthy kitchen.

By the 1950s, ideas about kitchen hygiene and labour-saving were firmly linked. In the absence of domestic servants the housewife had assumed the role of frontline warrior in the battle against evil germs. As cleanliness became ever more commercialised she was expected to achieve increasingly high standards. In magazines and home-making manuals everyday tasks came under the spotlight of 'expert' opinion with warnings that 'improper' washing-up, for example, could turn utensils like forks and spoons into

The general rule of thumb for refrigerators was to allow about 1 cubic foot of storage per household member. This luxury model with a full-width freezer locker cost £100 12s. The stand-alone deep-freeze was barely seen in Britain at this time.

Despite the claims of advertisements like this one, few people considered it a priority to acquire a dishwasher. Ownership rose from 0.01 per cent of households in 1945 to 1.5 per cent in 1965.

potential means of spreading infection. Electric dishwashers had been available in the USA since 1914 but this was the first era to see their promotion in Britain. While advertisements promised to end 'sink slavery' and guarantee sparkling dishes in minutes they rarely included a price. Dishwashers were too expensive to have wide appeal and the claims for efficiency ultimately proved too good to be true. Cheaper by far were the new proprietary, often synthetic, cleaning products first produced on a large scale after the Second World War. Squezy, the 'washup wizard', needed 'no measuring or shaking ... just pick up and squeeze [for] lots of energy-packed suds ... *No need to rinse or wipe.*' With a Goldilocks

The 1950s witnessed a shift towards branded cleaning products. Packaging like that seen here used strong colours to attract the housewife, with rival washing powders trying to outdo each other for the whitest whites.

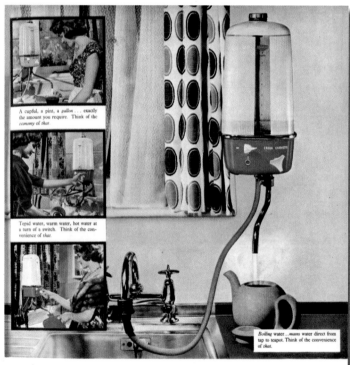

A cupful, a pint, a *gallon* ... exactly the amount you require. Think of the *economy of that.*

Tepid water, warm water, hot water at a turn of a switch. Think of the convenience of *that.*

Boiling water...*means* water direct from tap to teapot. Think of the convenience of *that.*

Water heaters were often seen above the sinks of 1950s kitchens. The lady in this advert is using her Creda Corvette for cooking, washing up and filling a hot water bottle.

Boiling water on tap...with this NEW Creda electric kitchen appliance

THE SMART little Creda Corvette, trimly mounted on wall or window-sill, gives you all these things and lots you see what goes on. You watch the water rising to the required level. You can actually watch it boil. It even tells you by means of a pilot light when it is tepid, warm or hot ... whatever heat you've set it to. And it's fast ... *very* fast. It boils a pint, for instance, in less than two minutes.

The Creda Corvette makes any kind of kettle pretty old-fashioned. For it is neither a kettle nor a water heater, but something *quite new;* it's a *Corvette* ... a hundred times more useful, economical and convenient. And it's so easy to clean—*inside.*

It is simple to fix, and there are no plumbing installation charges. It's British, and it's made by CREDA ... first in the field again.

Available in Red or Turquoise **£10-7-0d** plus P.T. £2.5.6d. *(pre budget)*

SIMPLEX ELECTRIC CO. LTD., CREDA WORKS, BLYTHE BRIDGE, STAFFS
LONDON SHOWROOMS: CREDA HOUSE, BINNEY STREET, W.1.

metal sponge the housewife was assured of the 'most up-to-date scouring' and for cleaner floors there was a new generation of effortless mops on the market, their cellulose sponge heads wrung out by a waist-high lever on the plastic handle that meant no more wet hands, bending or stooping.

It was in the labour-intensive task of home laundry, however, that women were most eager to invest their money in 1950s kitchen technology. It says much for the back-breaking toil of the weekly wash that machines which still required a great deal of manual intervention were so highly desirable. Actual washing time may have been reduced to a matter of minutes but as machines

Laundry put into the Burco Three-Ten could be boiled, but, to move it around, a hand-operated agitator unit had to be purchased separately. This model did at least have an automatic pump to remove waste water in under 3½ minutes.

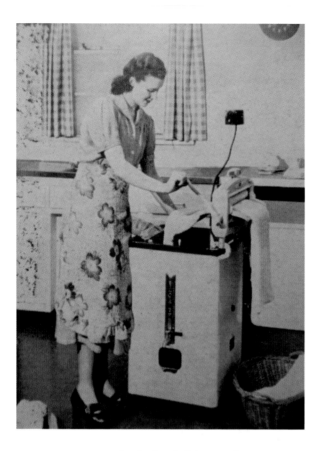

were not plumbed in they had to be moved over to the kitchen sink for filling from a bucket or pipe. After the power-driven 'agitation' of clothes was complete each wet item had to be individually passed through a hand-turned wringer. The machine then had to be emptied of water, pumps for this purpose coming in only gradually. Twin-tubs shared some of these drawbacks but the second tub for spinning and rinsing made them an increasingly popular choice by the end of the decade. In her autobiography *The House in South Road*, Joyce Storey recalls how a Hoover salesman arrived at her Bristol prefab one wash day in 1952 and, having made a promise to complete her laundry within an hour, wheeled in a demonstration twin-tub which did just that. It took much longer to convince

Unlike a mangle, which also had an ironing function, the wringer simply squeezed moisture out of wet laundry. This one was an integral part of the washing machine but separate sink wringers were also available.

her husband of the miracle Joyce had witnessed but it was essential because at that time only men were legally permitted to sign the forms for a hire-purchase loan.

For all their faults, washing machines did help make life easier for the 1950s housewife who could afford one. The next step up was an automatic clothes dryer. Noting the appearance in 1958 of the twelfth British spin dryer on the market, home columnist Alice Hope prophesied that 'the lines of washing flapping in the breezes of Britain's back yards ... are a disappearing feature of our countryside.' Though too costly to be common, early heated 'tumbler driers' were also obtainable. To complete the up-dating of laundry equipment, steam irons hit the shops in 1953–4, Mr Ken Wood bringing the original inventors over from the United States to ensure the success of his Steam-O-Matic model, made in Britain but 'Tested, Approved and Applauded by 3 million American housewives'. There was always a healthy dose of scepticism in the British response to new technology: convincing housewives that the new breed of ultra-light irons could be as satisfactory as heavier models took time, even though the latter required unnecessary extra labour. Reservations about individual products notwithstanding, the 1950s kitchen was well on its way to becoming the home of modern appliances that we recognise today.

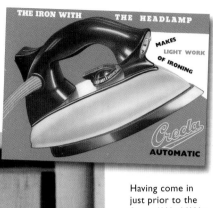

Having come in just prior to the Second World War, thermostatic controls were a universal feature of irons by 1960. The Creda 'Halo' was, however, the 'only British-made iron with a headlamp'.

Where there was limited outdoor space the rotary dryer with plastic-covered clothes line was a welcome 1950s innovation. For the housewife who wished to be independent of the weather there were heated drying cabinets like these.

Here is the latest addition to the Harper Housewares range — a beautifully stream-lined food mincer which every housewife will desire. Finished in gleaming green-mottle vitreous enamel that is easy to clean and absolutely hygienic. The special rubber-cushioned clamp will not damage your table top. The long handle and polished and hardened steel cutters make mincing effortless and efficient.

★*Your ironmonger or hardware dealer can show you this won-derful new mincer*

HARPER

Nº 1000

FOOD MINCER

"The very best"

HARPER HOUSEWARES

COOKWARE AND GADGETS

L ABOUR-SAVING appliances represented a big investment but there was also a multitude of smaller products developed throughout the 1950s which aimed to improve the housewife's efficiency in the core kitchen task of food preparation. Gadgets powered by electricity played an important part in the post-war campaign to increase domestic supply and, although there were few truly new inventions, the rise in consumer spending stimulated competition between manufacturers and led to improvements in design. Advertisements and magazine articles pictured fitted kitchens replete with these accessories reinforcing the idea that modern kitchens were filled with modern utensils. If the co-ordinated units were out of reach, such images provided a ray of hope by inferring that the purchase of less expensive items could provide a way into the modern kitchen vision.

Vegetables could be chopped with stainless steel knives that were much easier to clean than their predecessors, while potatoes could be prepared automatically with devices such as the Merry-Go Home Potato Peeler advertised in 1952 as capable of peeling 'up to 3lbs potatoes or root vegetables, just at the turn of a handle'. Mincers had been used since the nineteenth century and in the 1957 Newnes book of *Household Management* still came under the heading of indispensable 'miscellaneous articles'. Devices like this relied upon mechanical hand operation but that did not stop manufacturers from making claims for greater efficiency. The Prestige egg beater 'does *all* the beating jobs in the kitchen, quicker and without effort ... Thanks to smooth, easy running gears and eight stainless steel blades that beat faster! It's the perfect gift for the busy housewife.'

Even better was the electric liquidiser or blender, which rendered the old-fashioned sieve near superfluous by its ability to make a smooth vegetable or fruit purée in seconds. Most covetable of all gadgets, however, was the electric food mixer. The leading American model was the Sunbeam Mixmaster but in 1950 the hugely successful Kenwood Chef was launched. Ministry of Food guru Marguerite Patten gave demonstrations at Harrods department store while Kenwood-trained personnel were sent out to carefully selected

Opposite: Housewives purchasing fitted units were advised to make sure that worktops had sufficient ledge space to secure a mincer like this one. The streamlined Harper No. 1000 had a rubber-cushioned clamp and hardened steel cutters to make mincing 'effortless and efficient'.

Right: These Sky-line utensils were designed
to be seen, their brand name resonant of
an era that began with erection of the
futuristic Festival of Britain Skylon on
London's South Bank.

Below left: This Kenwood Chef food mixer
was given to the author's grandparents on
their marriage in 1950. Attachments
included a 'K' mixer and whisk (seen here),
a dough hook, fruit juice extractor, meat
mincing and vegetable chopping unit,
liquidiser attachment, colander and sieve.

Below right: Taking its design cue from
streamlined American automobiles and
aeroplanes, the Sunbeam Mixmaster had
a swivelling tailfin inscribed with the precise
settings for each of its many functions.
It came in standard white, pink, yellow,
turquoise and chrome.

dealers in the provinces. The company's marketing material emphasised the Chef's efficiency, multi-purpose functionality and design 'for speed and simplicity in use. It is elegant in appearance and beautifully streamlined, and – of great importance – it employs a planetary action as used in large industrial mixing plants.' Because of a range of attachments, the list of 'wrist-aching jobs' it could carry out at the 'flick of a switch' was impressively long. It could mix pastry, puddings and cakes, whip cream, whisk batters, make mayonnaise, knead dough, mash potatoes, mince meat, grind coffee, extract juice, chop raw vegetables or turn them straight into a cream soup. At £28 6s 0d it was expensive, but that just added to the aspirational appeal.

Salter Domestic Balance Scale, c. 1950. Measuring out ingredients was simplified by new scales with plastic trays and clear round dials. These did away with separate weights, making the process more accurate.

In December 1952 Kenwood ran an advertising campaign in middle-class home and women's magazines, claiming to divulge the secret of 'Why American Housewives look younger!' Their *jeunesse* was apparently down to widespread use of the electric food mixer and so 'It is of special – and exciting – interest to know … that even American women agree that the greatest of all electric mixers is the British "Chef", by Kenwood.' This was no idle boast. At the end of August 1953 the liner *Mauretania* set sail for America carrying £60,000 worth of Kenwood Chef mixers in its hold, prompting the triumphant *Daily Express* by-line 'Gadgets from Britain go to gadget-land'. This success was all the more remarkable as the company set up by 36-year-old Kenneth Wood had achieved a turnover of £1 million within the space of just seven years. After the war, Wood set up his first 'factory' next to a fish shop in Woking, beginning with toasters because they were cheap to produce. The Chef mixer, its prototype parts turned on a borrowed lathe in a garden shed, gave him his big break. In 1953 it was followed by the Kenwood Minor, a portable food mixer costing less than £10 and designed to hang on a wall bracket when not in use. The firm's product range quickly expanded into other domestic appliances, as well as cooking gadgets such as the electric egg poacher and the electric rotisserie, launched in 1957.

The ultimate cooking device of the period was the pressure cooker, which appeared in a revolutionary lightweight form from 1948. Its specially sealed unit captures and controls the steam that escapes from a normal saucepan, causing a rise in

Mrs Dorothy Hedges pictured with her new Kenwood Chef. Like many 1950s kitchens, hers was a mix of old and new, with deep stoneware butler's sink alongside her washing machine.

Presto COOKERS

Presto **MODEL 604**
THE COOK-MASTER
Made of Pressed Aluminium. Has
⅛" thick base, similar in size to 404.

Presto **MODEL 404**
THE COOK-MASTER
Made of Cast Aluminium. Suitable
for the smaller family.

Presto **MODEL 406**
THE MEAT-MASTER
Made of Cast Aluminium. Popular
family model.

Presto **MODEL 407**
THE FOOD-MASTER
Similar to the Presto Model 406,
except that it is fitted with a deep
lid to enable 2-lb. preserving jars
to be accommodated.

pressure that increases the boiling point of water inside. That high pressure then forces the super-heated steam through the food, cooking it much faster than usual. The basic principle had been known since the seventeenth century but old-fashioned 'digesters' were too large and heavy for everyday use. Post-war models made of aluminium and stainless steel were enthusiastically welcomed, not least for their economy at a time when the country was still subject to severe fuel cuts. A beef stew that would conventionally take 2½ hours to cook could be ready in just 15 minutes while the steamed

Above: Pressure cooking offered many advantages for the post-war housewife. Food retained its natural flavour and colour as well as its healthy minerals and vitamins.

Pots and pans were now decorative and colourful as well as practical and labour-saving. This selection from the Mirroware range featured red plastic handles. The unusually shaped pan on the right is the Mirromagic 'can't boil over' milk pan.

pudding so beloved of British families would take 35 minutes instead of 1½ hours. In fact, a whole meal could be prepared using just one hob because 'different kinds of foods, even those as highly flavoured as onions, can be cooked in the same cooker at the same time as pudding or fruit without the slightest danger of contamination'. Until the proliferation of convenience foods in the 1960s it was *the* modern way of cooking.

Aluminium had been used for saucepans since the 1920s but during the war housewives had been asked to contribute their precious cooking pots for the 1940 'Saucepans into Spitfires' propaganda drive. In the 1950s these mundane items got the contemporary treatment with the addition of coloured plastic knobs and handles. Crown Merton advertised aluminium

Jetware kitchen products were made from vitreous enamel glass-on-steel and came in a range of multi-coloured designs.

An example of Pyrex Opal ware, this oblong casserole dish has been screen-printed with the 'Daisy' pattern on a pink ground. It was marketed from 1958 as part of the 'Gaiety' range.

With their distinctive stubby handles, the ceramic oven-to-tablewares produced by Swedish company Rörstrands had the extra cachet of an import. British equivalents were made by Denby pottery.

pans 'designed by artist craftsmen', without which 'no kitchen is really modern'. Even cast-iron pans got a revamp: Izons & Co of West Bromwich promised perfect cooking from a contemporary range of pots that 'are finished in attractive colours, are easy to clean and handle and have a machined base which will not warp'. Non-stick coatings were not introduced to Britain until 1967, so anything that minimised scrubbing was a distinct selling point.

Oven-to-tableware also saved on washing up because the same dishes could be used for cooking *and* serving. The American Corning Glass Works began to manufacture domestic products from heat-resistant borosilicate glass as early as 1915, licensing their Pyrex trademark to the Sunderland firm J. A. Jobling in 1921. The brand's reputation was well established by the 1950s and gained fresh impetus from the employment of a company designer in 1951. Two years later Pyrex introduced the 'Easy-grip' range of casseroles with Opal 'Tableware' finding a ready market from 1957. Its glittery white surface could be coloured and decorated like china but had added strength and heat resistance to recommend it. Competing product lines were manufactured by the Phoenix Glassworks at Bilston. Ceramic oven dishes were also available and, in her

1951 book of *French Country Cooking*, Elizabeth David advocated earthenware for its attractive look as well as the flavour it added to food.

The Sunbeam 'Automatic Frypan' was certainly not Mrs David's style but it had its fans when it hit the market in 1956. One journalist reprimanded British manufacturers for failing to exploit demand:

> Since the war, when American magazines returned to our bookstalls, we have stopped in awe at the page advertising this automatic electrical frypan, joy of the American housewife and the one-room career girl. Whenever a British electric gadget manufacturer has asked us what the women of Britain want, we have shouted THE AUTOMATIC FRYPAN! They nodded politely and looked suspicious.

Promoted as the ultimate convenience, it could be plugged in and set to cook directly on the table, the addition of a lid transforming it into a roaster, boiler and baker. The temperature was easily controlled by a switch on the handle and as the heating element was sealed into the main body the entire pan could be washed. Futuristic though it seemed, this was one gadget that failed to become an indispensable tool in the British kitchen.

Other portable plug-ins found a mass market where they had previously been used only by the rich. The first electric kettles proved desperately slow to boil when they were invented in the United States in 1893. A survey by the Electrical Association for Women showed that there were still problems in 1950, respondents asking for faster boiling, better protection from steam and a flatter element so that the kettle did not always have to be full. Over the ensuing decade improvements were made. Whistles finally solved the problem of knowing when the water was hot enough and sales of singing kettles substantially increased after 1955. Cut-out devices also became more common. Electric toasters had been available since the 1920s but the single central element meant bread had to be watched and turned by hand. In the 1950s new automatic models appeared, complete with neat rounded ends. Other innovations included the first fully automatic electrically powered coffee percolator with keep-hot device invented in the early 1950s by Bill Russell and Peter Hobbs, and the waffle maker in the shape of a flying saucer on show at the 1950–1 Ideal Home Exhibition.

Any gadget or appliance that could be set to function automatically was given the 'robot' label. Toasters such as this were a distinct improvement on the old type, in which bread had to be turned by hand.

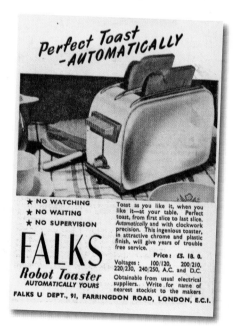

Perfect Toast
— AUTOMATICALLY

★ NO WATCHING
★ NO WAITING
★ NO SUPERVISION

FALKS

Robot Toaster
AUTOMATICALLY YOURS

Toast as you like it, when you like it—at your table. Perfect toast, from first slice to last slice. Automatically and with clockwork precision. This ingenious toaster, in attractive chrome and plastic finish, will give years of trouble free service.

Price: £5. 18. 0.

Voltages: 100/120, 200/210, 220/230, 240/250, A.C. and D.C.

Obtainable from usual electrical suppliers. Write for name of nearest stockist to the makers

FALKS U DEPT., 91, FARRINGDON ROAD, LONDON, E.C.1.

FIFTIES FOOD

THE SHIFT from austerity to prosperity was visible in all areas of life but perhaps especially so in the different food choices available at the beginning and end of the 1950s. Post-war global food shortages meant a slow transition back to normality with continued rationing until 1954. By the end of the decade, however, cookery books were full of fancy and exotic-sounding meal ideas with brightly coloured pictures that confirmed the bad old days were just that. The healthy but highly restrictive wartime diet had left little room for the social rituals associated with food, but these returned as soon as practically possible. Entertaining was definitely back on the 1950s menu. For everyday eating the introduction of new processed foods demonstrated that even nutrition could be made labour saving in the efficient modern kitchen.

The archetypal housewife of 1950s advertising was, by extension, a fabulous cook. Yet many young women began married life lacking the practical experience to live up to this stereotype. Like their husbands-to-be, they had often gone straight from school into war work or the forces, eating communally in factory canteens and subsidised British restaurants without the benefit of seeing how food was prepared. Notwithstanding this shared experience, there remained an expectation that the new wife would have an innate ability to achieve the culinary standards of her mother-in-law, offering up meals just the way her husband liked them. Ultimately it was money and inclination that determined a wife's response to the needs of feeding a growing family. Among members of the baby boomer generation there are those who recall a fairly static weekly menu of traditional dishes that mother could afford and had perfected. Sunday was roast beef and Yorkshire pudding, cold meat followed the day after, and you knew it was Wednesday when the plate of sausages and mashed potato appeared on the table.

Whatever culinary level she desired to achieve, there were plentiful sources of instruction aimed at the housewife. Magazine publishing experienced a heyday in the 1950s and cookery features were a staple of female home-making titles. The best-selling weekly was *Woman*, whose typical

Opposite:
In May 1954 butter, margarine and cooking fats finally came off ration. Puff pastry was time-consuming to make and had been impossible during the Second World War but adventurous hostesses could now attempt showy food like vol-au-vents.

Cooking was an everyday task too mundane to capture the interest of photographers, so images like this, of an ordinary woman at her stove, are very rare.

Almost every foodstuff had its own post-war marketing board. In 1942 eggs were rationed to one per person per week, often being replaced in cooking by reconstituted dried eggs. After de-rationing in 1953 leaflets such as this one reminded people of their versatility.

reader – young and married, with two children but not a lot of money – was invited to join the magazine's 'Wooden Spoon Club', launched early in the decade. Recipe leaflets were also widely produced by food producers and their marketing boards. Day and evening classes were popular and well-attended, on top of which there were the television cooks who brought their step-by-step recipes into an increasing number of homes. The Coronation of Queen Elizabeth II on 2 June 1953 prompted a discernible spike in television sales and those well-off enough to have made the investment kept 'open house', sharing the optimistic celebrations with friends and neighbours, often over a lunchtime buffet that included the dish of the day, Coronation Chicken. By 1965, 85 per cent of households owned a television compared to just 0.25 per cent twenty years earlier. Favourite cook Marguerite Patten made her reputation on radio, with regular and trusted contributions to the BBC wartime programme *Kitchen Front*. From her first television appearance in 1947 she helped steer the country's taste buds beyond rationing and her demonstrations of how to make, marzipan and ice a Christmas cake in 1952 seemed to mark a turning point on the road to better times. From the middle of the decade her role was cemented through presidency of the BBC Television 'Cookery Club', an afternoon institution in which she set viewers a weekly challenge. After testing the submissions herself, Patten invited the winning housewife to discuss the recipes with her, live in the studio. Self-taught chef Philip Harben also carved out a successful niche as a writer and presenter with his BBC *Cookery* series running from 1946 to 1951, followed by *What's Cooking?* from 1956.

ADD AN EGG AND COOK STILL BETTER

New collection of add-an-egg ideas for everyone in the family

For those who already knew how to cook, such programmes offered ideas on how to enhance existing skills, working towards that mythical 1950s status of the perfect hostess. Entertaining on limited rations was difficult but, as the vogue for cocktail parties proved, it was possible. Attractively presented savoury snacks disguised the privations of the late 1940s and early 1950s, which would have been obvious at a full dinner party, while the cocktails themselves added a touch of much needed glamour. Reason to rejoice came with the abolition of the tea ration in February 1952, after which Marguerite Patten received a rush of requests for cake and biscuit recipes to be served at special tea parties. As the quantities of fat and sugar available for use in baking returned to normal in the second half of the decade, women went to town, laying out their best embroidered tablecloths and tea sets for guests, ready to present that symbol of womanliness, the perfect Victoria sponge. Cake-making became a matter of feminine pride as recipe books offered ever fancier variations with bright and complicated icing schemes; the 1958 *Good Housekeeping Cookery Compendium* included a bewildering array of cakes decorated to look like mushrooms! Food presentation took on a new importance, subject to fashion in a way that directly challenged scarcities of the recent past.

Fanny Cradock's television programmes of the late 1950s typified this gleeful extravagance. Whilst assuring viewers that 'this won't stretch your purse', she named every dish in French and built a television persona as heavily garnished as her food. This was the era of soufflés, flambés and gateaux.

Philip Harben in his trademark uniform of shirt and tie with striped butcher's apron tied at the waist. Like fellow cook and friend Marguerite Patten, Harben was well suited to his television role as part entertainer, part teacher.

Sandwich cutters like these were designed to meet the demand for novelty presentation that was a hallmark of 1950s party food.

The Stork Margarine Cookery Service offered free advice on all cooking problems, issuing booklets like this one on how to bake perfect cakes. Women who lacked the time to hone this feminine art could increasingly cheat with shop-bought cake mixes.

Dips were an innovation at the buffet table and citrus fruits, once prized for their rarity, were now wasted in the prickled display of cocktail sticks. The 1957 Newnes book of *Household Management* counselled that 'the appearance of a dish is every bit as important as its vitamin content and its flavour, for it is the appeal to the eye that tempts the appetite'. Decoration with sculpted gherkins, petal-cut tomato halves (there was even a product called the 'Tomat-O-Matic' for precision cutting) or maraschino cherries could transform an otherwise ordinary meal. 'When you dish up roast duck, surround it on the dish with slices of fresh, peeled orange and lettuce leaves; the contrast in flavour as well as colour is memorable, the kind of little details that mark you out as a hostess of ideas.'

Every competitive advantage had to be exploited for that high point of socialising, the dinner party – whether it was a question of keeping up with the Joneses, impressing the husband's boss or entertaining his clients. Yet the impact of a good display was not restricted to the food. Well-placed gadgets in an up-to-date kitchen helped give the right impression while the wife played her part by appearing in the sort of 'hostess dress' recommended by magazines, often complete with full skirts for the glamorous Doris Day look. Over the top her work-a-day apron was replaced by a flimsier, frilled version, the very impracticality of which belied the true

The 1950s saw a rage for setting anything and everything in aspic. It was partly wartime thriftiness that made people look for new ways to use up leftovers. Here diced cold meat is combined in aspic with peas and egg slices for colour.

Recipe books were full of photographs that explained the preparation steps alongside finished dishes. This close-up shows how to 'vandyke' the edge of a grapefruit prior to garnishing with petals of fresh or frosted mint.

amount of effort required in preparing the meal. Finally there was the hostess trolley, heated electrically or with night lights in the chromium frame, designed to be wheeled in by the fashionable housewife so that food arrived piping hot at the table.

As imports of exotic produce rose, traditional British fare was joined on the menu by more cosmopolitan offerings. The war had given people confidence to be more adventurous in their tastes, both as a result of meeting allied forces or refugees on the home front and because so many British men and women gained first-hand knowledge of foreign cuisines whilst serving abroad. The number of Britons holidaying on the Continent also rose, from 900,000 in 1950 to 2 million in 1958. Though her influence was initially restricted to the educated middle classes, no one captured the essential link between place and food better than Elizabeth David, who began her publishing career with *A Book of Mediterranean Food* in 1949. Over the ensuing decade she collected recipes from the country kitchens of France and Italy, bringing them to life in her evocative writings and never compromising on ingredients, despite the difficulties of obtaining them outside of Soho delicatessens. Courgettes, aubergines and red and green peppers gradually crept into shops and one magazine recommended a garlic squeezer as the perfect cook's present for Christmas 1954: 'It will help give the Continental touch to all kinds of dishes.' Imports of corn-on-the-cob rose dramatically in the early 1950s, 'largely due to the demand for it by visiting Americans', and in 1956 Philip Harben assured readers of his *Woman's Own* 'Cookery School' that, although avocado pears were said to be an acquired taste, 'it doesn't take more than a few seconds to acquire it!'

If one mark of post-war modernity was a willingness to experiment with new cooking ingredients, the other, contrary, shift was towards more pre-prepared convenience foods. Even traditional staples were not immune from labour-saving spin: an advertisement in July 1956 promised 'Time off for housewives … thanks to cheese'! During the war bread had been rationed and bakers could sell only the 'National Loaf' made with 85 per cent wholemeal flour. After restrictions were lifted huge new bakery plants were built to make light and fluffy white bread wrapped in enticing brand names such as Sunblest, Mother's Pride and Wonder Loaf. Marketers encouraged the

Worn for centuries to protect clothes from dirt, the humble apron was appropriated as an emblem of the perfect 1950s hostess. Ubiquitous in advertising images, flimsy fashion aprons like this one implied hard kitchen labour was a thing of the past.

idea that time saved by making a cheese sandwich with pre-sliced bread could be dedicated to the far more interesting pursuit of watching television. In 1957 Lin-Can suggested ways of turning its range of tinned foods into appetising snacks perfect for what it called 'the "spoon or fork" meal, eaten not at table but from a tray upon the knees. One can eat and watch at the same time when there is no knife to manipulate.' Advertisements for newly invented Nescafé promised instant coffee that was 'So quick to make – you don't miss a thing' and in 1953 Tetley introduced the time-saving tea bag. No lesser sign of things to come was the rapid rise of frozen foods. Mr Clarence

Right:
A Mediterranean feast as envisaged by Lincolnshire Canners Ltd. 'Best before' dates had yet to be introduced, so housewives were advised to label their tins with the date of purchase and use the oldest first.

Opposite:
Sweets came off ration in February 1953 followed by sugar in September. By the end of the decade the British sweet tooth was being indulged to the tune of 57 kg of sugar per capita per year, second only to Greenland.

Birdseye's innovative 'quick freezing' process was introduced to Britain from the United States, leading to the first mass pea harvest in 1946, 390 tonnes being frozen that year at the company's factory in Great Yarmouth. It was there, nine years later, that the much-loved fish finger was born.

Between 1955 and 1960 the frozen food market increased by more than 500 per cent with Birds Eye leading the way. By renting cabinet freezers to retailers the company could supply a rapidly expanding range of vegetables, fruit, fish, meat and pies.

"ISN'T THERE A LOT TO CHOOSE FROM, MUM!"

stop at your Birds Eye Shop

BIRDS EYE SHOP

Even the act of *buying* food began to alter. At the end of the 1940s Jack Cohen, co-founder of Tesco, was one of the first British shop owners to follow the self-service model set in the pre-war United States. In 1950 Sainsbury's turned its Croydon branch 'Q-less', beginning its move from supplying groceries that were cut and wrapped on request to the modern retailing standard of pre-packaged goods picked by the customers themselves. Looking to the future, Newnes book of *Household Management* commented on how 'Self-service shops are becoming complete shopping centres … The housewife can take her basket-on-wheels … and buy a week's provisions, plus cigarettes and cosmetics if she wishes. And *everything* is wrapped.' Innovations in the 1950s kitchen, whether in design, appliances or the food consumed there, were all linked to broader social changes that have shaped the way we live today.

The traditional small shop where people waited for individual counter service began to be challenged by a new breed of self-service stores. By 1956 the Co-operative Society operated more than three thousand, including this one at Stevenage New Town.

FURTHER READING

Burnett, John. *A Social History of Housing 1815–1970*. Methuen, 1978.

Conran, Terence. *Kitchens Past and Present: A Guide to Their Evolution, Planning and Decoration*. Hygena Ltd, 1976.

Good Housekeeping. *The Best of the 1950s*. Collins & Brown, 2008.

Hardyment, Christina. *Slice of Life: The British Way of Eating Since 1945*. BBC Books, 1995.

Hoskins, Lesley. *Fiftiestyle: Home Decoration and Furnishings from the 1950s*. MODA, Middlesex University Press, 2004.

Jackson, Lesley. *'Contemporary' Architecture and Interiors of the 1950s*. Phaidon, 1999.

Leighton, Sophie. *The 1950s Home*. Shire, 2009.

Lewin, Susan Grant (editor). *Formica and Design: From the Counter Top to High Art*. Rizzoli, 1991.

MacDonald, Sally, and Porter, Julia. *Putting on the Style: Setting up Home in the 1950s*. The Geffrye Museum, 1990.

Marsh, Madeleine. *Miller's Collecting the 1950s*. Octopus, 2004.

Patten, Marguerite. *Post-War Kitchen: Nostalgic Food and Facts from 1945–54*. Past Times, 1998.

Pressley, Alison. *The Best of Times: Growing Up in Britain in the 1950s*. Past Times/Michael O'Mara Books, 1999.

Yarwood, Doreen. *The British Kitchen*. Batsford, 1981.

Website:
www.makingthemodernworld.org.uk

With all its up-to-date appliances the 1950s kitchen came to symbolise post-war modernity

Two magnificent MAIN refrigerators

THE MAIN 36C
A 36 cu. ft. refrigerator of distinction completely re-designed to give 7·7 sq. ft. shelf area and with full width frozen food locker. Available electric or gas. Still the *only* refrigerator with a 10 YEAR GUARANTEE on its sealed cooling unit. You deserve a MAIN 36C!
Price £63.10.0 TAX PAID

THE MAIN 22
A compact, multi-feature 2·2 cu. ft. refrigerator for the smaller kitchen, at a price to please *everyone's* pocket! Door shelves include capacity for 4 pints of milk. Available electric, or gas. 5 YEAR GUARANTEE on sealed cooling unit. Outstanding value for
43 guineas TAX PAID

R. & A. MAIN LTD. 48 GROSVENOR GARDENS, LONDON S.W.1

INDEX